Steve Milano & Associates, LLC
110 Roswell Farms Lane
Roswell, GA 30075

Steve Milano

First Edition

ISBN 978-0615589145

Printed in United States of America

# Survival Guide for Managing Corporate Fatigue

*How to Reduce Physical and Mental Stress Through Habit and Lifestyle Changes*

# Contents

# Foreword

I used to spend the night at a friend's apartment in Chicago, and the room I slept in was awful for trying to sleep. The room overlooked one of the city's busiest intersections, where five high-traffic streets met. Directly underneath the window of this second-floor apartment was a bus stop. All night long, buses would whoosh into their stops, open their doors, discharge and take on passengers, then whoosh away.

Across the street was a pay-before-you-pump gas station. New customers would try to start pumping and the clerk would get on the loudspeaker and blast, "Sir, you need to come inside and pay first!," jolting me out of bed.

And it got worse. On the windowsill, about 10 feet from my head, pigeons would congregate, softly cooing. The windows had sheer curtains that, combined with a skylight, inundated the room with bright sunshine each morning. Let's not even talk about how uncomfortable the bed was.

Despite all of these impediments to sound sleep, I woke up refreshed and ready to run a marathon each morning. I couldn't understand it. I usually hated getting up each morning. I slammed my hand on the alarm clock to shut it up. I walked to the bathroom with my eyes closed, mumbling under my breath. I dreaded facing the coming commute.

Why did I feel so good then, whenever I slept at my friend's apartment?

My friend told me, "I have a theory that if you wake up in a room with sunlight, you wake up feeling better."

So I tried it. The next night, back in my apartment, I raised my window shade open a bit before I went to bed. I preferred sleeping and waking in a pitch-dark room, but thought I'd give it a try.

Sure enough, the next morning I awoke without the usually grogginess and irritability I often experienced when the alarm clock went off. I didn't hate my boss, job or clients that morning.

What happened?

As humans evolved physiologically during our history, whenever our eyes saw darkness coming, our brains registered it as a signal to sleep. For most of human history, man did not have light — not even fire. So after dark, we went into our caves and slept. When it got dark, our brains released the hormone melatonin to help us sleep better. As our brains experienced sunlight the next morning, the melatonin production slowed and we were no longer sleepy.

When you wake in a pitch-dark room, your brain is swimming in melatonin because it thinks you want to keep sleeping. You wake up drowsy, groggy, irritable and not in a positive mood to start you day. You shave, shower, brush your teeth or dress with your eyes half open. You can dread going into work and want to get back into bed.

If, on the other hand, you wake up in a brightly lit room, your brain will have slowed melatonin production and you are more likely to get out of bed refreshed and ready to go.

This simple lifestyle change can make a huge difference in your life.

Yes, trying to sleep with sunlight in your eyes is no fun, so consider how you'll arrange your curtains to light your room each morning. If it's still dark outside when you get up in the morning, purchase a lamp with a timer that slowly turns on, raising the room's light level 15 minutes or so before you want to wake.

You don't need to make major lifestyles changes to make major improvements to your life. Small but regular changes in your daily habits are easy to make and pay huge dividends. These changes can help you become more alert, more productive each hour you work and less likely to have high blood pressure, a heart attack, stroke, depression, anger or other physical and mental problems.

This book is filled with tips for improving your eating, sleeping, fitness and stress-management habits.

You don't need to eat tofu and sprouts, meditate and chant or exercise for 90 minutes each day to completely change your life for the better.

This book gives you quick overviews of areas of your life you can modify – not completely change – to improve your business performance and personal life.

•If you're going to eat at fast-food restaurants, there are ways to do it so it's not as unhealthy.

•There are ways to get meaningful exercise without going to the gym.

•There are ways to reduce your stress levels without yoga and TM.

There's nothing wrong with committing to serious diet, fitness and stress-management programs, but if you feel that is not for you, modifying (not completely changing) your habits can still change your life.

If you can't live healthy, at least live healthier.

It's easier than you know, will make you more productive and successful in business and life, can ward off diseases, conditions and even death for many years . . . and might even be fun for you.

# Chapter I:
# Sleep Habits

Going without sleep or with little sleep is not too bright . . . even during short-term project deadlines.

There may be times you don't have a choice, but if you regularly pull all-nighters or work on only a few hours of sleep, you'll decrease the quantity and quality of the work you do each day and begin to damage your brain and body.

The hours of extra work you put in when you're tired not only are less valuable than those you perform when you're adequately rested, but you'll also increase your risk of an error, which can result in a lost client or financial damage to your company.

You also significantly increase your chances of mental and physical problems if you regularly get insufficient sleep.

Why? Your body is made up of millions of cells, which are stressed and damaged each day. When you sleep, your body repairs these cells. Your heart rate slows as this important muscle recovers; your blood pressure goes down; your body temperature decreases; your brain releases hormones differently allowing your body to better regulate itself.

Sleep repairs the damage you do to your body during the day. Lack of sleep can also make you less productive during the day. You may be working those extra hours because you don't produce as much work per hour as you do when you are rested. This can be the result of the decreased cognitive and memory functions that come from lack of sleep. The quality of your work may suffer as you miss important details, fail to come up with new ideas or miss possible solutions to problems.

The quality of hours you put in each day outweighs the quantity of hours you work.

# Are you an Early Bid or a Night Owl?

Some people love to get to the office early, doing their best work before most people have even arrived. Others are still dead at their desk until 10:00 am, finding their stride later and working at a feverish pace late at night.

A brain hormone may play a role in when you work best.

Noradrenaline, also known as norepinephrine, helps stimulate your bodily functions. Some people produce more noradrenaline in the morning, while others produce more at night. Research suggests that most people fall in between these two extremes, performing their best during normal working hours. But if you feel you're an early bird or night owl, now you know why.

If you like to sleep in on the weekends, you're not necessarily lazy. If you can't work late at night, you're not a wimp. We all have productive periods during the day. Two people may be able to work the exact number of hours at the exact level of peak performance, even though one starts early in the morning and the other works in the evening.

If you have an extreme circadian rhythm, or body clock, and feel your best very early in the morning or very late at night, understand and respect this phenomenon. Save important tasks for your peak periods and take breaks or do lighter work during your down times.

Let key co-workers know your preferences so you can schedule your contribution to the team when you are performing at your best. For example, if you are a night owl, you may want to schedule internal meetings during morning hours, conducting important client research or analyses late at night when you are peaking. Let your co-workers know you'd rather do a less-important breakfast meeting than a dinner outing if you have an important project you need to finish that night. If you're an early bird, schedule breakfast meetings for important tasks or review sensitive documents when you first get into the office.

# How Much Sleep?

The National Sleep Foundation recommends at least eight hours of sleep each night for maximal mental and physical benefit. Some people believe they are best served with only six or seven hours of sleep, with some reporting grogginess or fatigue if they get more than that.

A lack of sleep not only affects your body, but your brain efficiency, as well. You may experience reduced verbal, cognitive and memory function. Your mood can move to irritability, stress, anger, frustration or depression. Long-term sleep deprivation can lead to brain damage and mental disorders because the enzymes that repair your brain during adequate sleep can't do their jobs.

# Power Napping

Many cultures include afternoon naps in their daily routine to help maintain good health. During late afternoon, when outdoor temperatures are highest, Latin populations siesta for an hour or two after a large lunch.

You don't need to lie down and take a 30-minute or hour-long snooze to benefit from napping. If you know you're going to be working late, tell your assistant to hold your calls, then close your office door and turn out the lights for 15 minutes and grab a nap in your chair. If you're making a cross-town cab trip back from a client, turn off your cell phone and catch a few Zs in the cab. Depending on how many time zones you'll be changing during a flight and which direction you'll be traveling, you may be better served by a nap during your flight than an extra 30 minutes of computer work.

If you are a manager and you are asking an employee or group of workers to work late into the night or pull an all-nighter, set up a time during the day for them to take a nap. They'll wake up refreshed and be more productive and able to stay up later during crunch time.

Some people hate naps. Instead of waking up refreshed, they experience headaches, grogginess, prolonged drowsiness and irritability. This could come from a number of reasons, such as very little sleep or too much sleep the night before; restless sleep due to stress; trying to sleep in a lit room; or a nap that's too short or too long.

If you don't like napping, don't give up on this important productivity tool. Experiment at home on the weekends, to see if you can determine what type of napping will help you. You may need a minimum of 30 minutes, need to nap in a dark room or nap only after you've had a good night's sleep.

One of the benefits of taking the train into work may be that you catch an extra 30 to 60 minutes of sleep each morning. If you can nap both ways, you might be able to add up to two hours of sleep to your daily routine.

## Regulate Your Light Source

Have you ever attended a lecture or presentation that included a slide show or PowerPoint presentation? What happened after the speaker asked for the room lights to be turned down so the audience could see the screen better? If you didn't soon become groggy, you probably noticed others in the audience passing out. This is because of the brain's reaction to darkness — increased melatonin production to help you sleep.

As noted in the introduction to this book, the amount of light your eyes register affects the amount of melatonin your body produces, and that makes you sleepy.

At home, set your curtains to ensure you have sunlight in your room when you wake. If you can't do that, consider a sleep lamp that turns on at a time you set.

Bring a sleep mask on work trips to use during flights and at hotels with curtains or drapes that let too much light in at night. Use a sleep mask at home if you have light from a parking lot light or neighbor's home streaming into your room.

# Regulate Your Room Temperature

Research suggests that a cooler room may help promote sleep. When you sleep, your body lowers its core temperature. This means sleeping in a cooler room may help you sleep better.

Keep your home or hotel room between 60 and 68 degrees F. Sleeping in a room colder than that may cause restlessness. If you share a room with someone who prefers it warm, you may need to compromise. You may need to sleep under only a sheet, rather than a blanket, while your partner may need to sleep in pajamas, a sweatshirt or other clothing.

If you are on a plane, skip using a blanket and use the overhead air conditioning nozzle if that won't irritate you.

Although your body lowers it overall temperature when you sleep, the temperature in your hands and feet rises. Sleeping with socks on, or putting your airline blanket around your feet when you fly, might help you sleep better. Wear synthetic, rather than cotton, socks when you sleep to keep your feet dry.

# Dealing with Jet Lag

Traveling across time zones can disrupt your body clock. This is truer when you change more than one or two time zones and spend more than a day or two out of town. Jet lag can produce sluggishness, drowsiness, decreased concentration, lack of alertness and reduce memory function.

For most people, traveling from New York to L.A. or vice versa for a day or two isn't that big a deal in terms of your overall productivity. You may be a bit drowsy when you arrive, have trouble falling asleep that first night or be tired when you wake up the next morning, but you can probably fight through this for the short time you're out of town with no ill effect. International travel creates more serious jet lag issues.

# Flying East to West

Let's say you leave New York, arriving in L.A. at 8:00 pm. It's 11:00 pm in New York, so you may be tired and ready for bed at 8:00 pm PST.

If you respect your current body clock and go to bed at 8:00 pm PST, waking up at 8:00 am the next morning, you'll have slept 12 hours. Many people who sleep this long feel extremely sluggish and lethargic. If you wake up naturally after eight hours of sleep, you'll wake up at 5:00 am. This will cause you to become sleepy again around 8:00 pm that evening.

If you sleep on the plane during your trip, you may not feel as sleepy when you arrive in L.A. at 8:00 pm. This will allow you to stay awake better until 11:00 pm PST (or your normal bed time). The trick is getting the right amount of sleep. If you get three hours of sleep, this might be too much. If you sleep for two hours, waking just before you land, this might keep you awake.

## *East-to-West Travel Tips*

•Sleep without a blanket to let your body lower its core temperature naturally, as it does when you sleep. You may fall asleep quicker and go into a deeper sleep.

•Wrap a blanket around your feet if the floor is drafty, since your body raises the temperature in your feet when you sleep.

•Close the window or wear a mask to keep light from your eyes.

•Stay hydrated. Travelers become dehydrated during flights because of the lack of humidity in the air. People also mistake dehydration for hunger and eat when they don't need to.

•Eat at least three to four hours before your in-flight nap. Eat more complex carbohydrates.

•Exercise several hours before you depart.

•Avoid caffeine and alcohol, which can lead to dehydration.

# Flying West to East

When you travel from the West Coast to the East Coast, you often arrive early in the morning. If your flight arrives as 1:00 am, EST, your body may feel like it's only 11:00 pm. If you've slept on the plane, it might seem even earlier, and you'll have trouble getting to sleep when you finally arrive home. When you attempt to get up at 8:00 am, you body might feel like it's still 5:00 am.

Even if you take a day flight, you might still have trouble getting to sleep later that night. When it's 11:00 pm EST, your body may still feel likes it's only 8:00 pm. If you slept on your flight, it might be even more difficult to get to sleep.

After a west-to-east flight, performing rigorous exercise during the afternoon or early evening may help you expend energy and sleep better that evening. If you get home during the day and want to stay awake, get out of your cab several blocks before your office or home and walk the final distance, raising your heart rate and metabolism. This will be especially helpful if it's a sunny day. If you can have breakfast outdoors in the sunlight in L.A., this might help you feel less sluggish when you arrive in New York than if you spend your West Coast morning hours in a cool, dark room.

It may be a good idea to sleep when it's nighttime in your destination zone. For example, if it's 9:00 pm PST while you're on your flight, it's 12:00 midnight in New York. You may want to sleep on your flight.

If you can get several hours of sleep, wake up after your plane lands, then quickly get back to sleep when you get home, it might be OK to "bank" some sleep hours on your flight. If you will be wired after you wake up from an in-flight nap, unable to get back to sleep after you arrive home from the airport, then avoid a nap. In this scenario, you might get home at 2:00 am, then have to get up after only 4 or 5 hours of sleep. Try banking sleep hours earlier in the day when you are on the West Coast to help you make up for this deficit.

## *West-to-East Travel Tips*

•Nap before you fly if you're arriving during the day.

•Open your windows if you're flying during the day.

•Eat during your flight if you're arriving during the day.

•Get outside in the warm and sunlight before you fly if you're flying during the day.

•Exercise after arriving if you're arriving during the day.

•Nap during the flight if you're arriving during the evening (if you won't be wired afterwards).

•Exercise before departing if you're arriving during the evening.

## Sleep Aids

The jury is out regarding just what medications you should take for sleep, how often you should take them and in what doses. Your situation may be due to stress, a time change or other conditions. One sleeping pill won't cure all sleep problems all the time. If you feel you need to take a sleep aid, talk to your doctor to determine what is best for you.

## Mattresses

You have many choices for mattresses, including hard, soft, water, self-molding, foam and coiled. Depending on whether you have any spinal or muscle problems, the best mattress for you may come down to simple preference. For most people, a firmer mattress is the best choice because it supports your spine better.

Always test a mattress before you buy. If you like a mattress at a particular hotel you visit, make a note of it. Be careful about falling in love with a mattress after one night's sleep. Your good sleep may have been the result of a variety of factors, including the amount of light in the room, exercise you performed earlier that day, lack of stress, the room temperature, lack of nearby noise, etc.

When was the last time you flipped your mattress? It's a good idea to flip and rotate your mattress every three months, similar to rotating your car tires. Mark one or all four corners or your mattress so you don't simply turn the mattress back and forth each time. If you don't flip your mattress, you'll end up sleeping with your head at one end and your feet on the other for the life of your mattress. If you want it to wear evenly, flip it the first time, then flip and turn it the second time, and so on, so that you sleep on all four areas of the bed.

## Pillows

Your pillows support your neck and head while you sleep, and after a time, they lose their ability to adequately support you. If you need to punch your pillow before you go to sleep each night to fluff it up, you may need to buy a new one.

If you sleep on your side, considers a thicker or firmer pillow to give you the support you need. If you sleep on your back or stomach, you may need less support.

When was the last time you washed your pillowcases and pillows? Pillows also absorb the oil, sweat and drool that leave your body at night. This attracts dust mites that can cause respiratory and allergy problems. If you have a large enough freezer, put your pillows inside for 12 hours to kill mites.

# Try White Noise

White noise consists of a sound or sounds you hear, but after a few minutes, don't really notice. For example, waves on a beach or steady rain without thunder or lightning are background sounds you get used to and they don't disturb your sleep. In fact, they can cover other noises that might disturb your sleep, such as traffic or animals outside. Buying a CD of white noise and playing it to get you to sleep may be an effective tool to help you fall asleep quicker, especially when you are in unfamiliar settings, such as a hotel or friend's or family member's home.

Some people sleep with the TV on as white noise. The light can adversely affect your sleep, so cover the screen or find out how to eliminate the picture. An older, larger TV can also raise the temperature in your room. Another problem is that while you may not consciously pay attention to what is coming from the TV, in your sleep state, the programming coming from the TV may affect your dreams. We often try to work out life problems in our dreams. Even if the TV content in your room isn't negative, you may dream about sports, exercise or cooking, rather than working out life situations you might otherwise contemplate if you weren't distracted by what's on your TV.

# Take a Break Before Bed

Don't go straight from your paperwork or computer to your bed and think you will get the same number of hours and quality of sleep. If your mind is racing after hours of problem-solving or difficult analytical tasks, you will not likely be able to quickly shut these thoughts off. It's best to knock off work at least 30 minutes before you intend to go to bed if you want to fall asleep faster. If you're going to watch some TV before you go to bed, avoid stressful programs, such as horror movies or the nightly news.

If you need to pack a suitcase, wash the dishes or do some other mundane task before you go to bed, save those tasks for after you are done working to give your mind a mental break before you hit the sack.

# Food and Sleep

There are no miracle foods that help you sleep. A popular myth promotes eating turkey, because it contains tryptophan, which helps get serotonin to the brain. There is not enough tryptophan in foods to have enough of an effect on your sleep. The real reason you fall asleep after Thanksgiving dinner has more to do with all the complex carbs you eat.

While carbohydrates don't have the same effect as a sleeping pill, they are better choices before a nap or night's sleep than protein or fat, because they do help get more serotonin to your brain. While you shouldn't look for foods to put you to sleep, you should avoid those that contain caffeine and sugar.

Does what you eat and when you eat it affect your ability to sleep? In short, yes. If you work late and eat when you get home, you may go to bed within an hour or two of your meal. This can make it more difficult to fall asleep and get into a deep restful sleep.

There are a variety of myths concerning eating late at night, most having to do with weight gain and fat storage. In a nutshell, the main problem with eating late at night or eating just before sleeping is that it can make restful sleep more difficult.

As far as weight gain and fat storage are concerned, it's how many total calories you eat during the day that is the key factor in weight gain. After that, how physically active you are determines how many calories you will burn. When you eat, then go to sleep, your sleep metabolism will affect your digestive process, but not how your body converts and processes calories.

When you eat a big meal, you may feel sleepy afterwards, but that's not because your body is slowing down. In actuality, your metabolism speeds up after you eat. Your circulatory system needs to move more blood, your stomach and pancreas secrete more gastric acid and digestive enzymes and your heart rate rises.

However, you may feel sleepy after a meal because your body has produced more serotonin in response to the carbohydrates you ate. Serotonin, like melatonin, helps you relax and sleep.

Caffeine in coffee, tea, sugary drinks, chocolate and spicy food interfere with sleep. If you drink coffee, tea or energy drinks to help keep you awake during late working hours, think what that will do to you when you finally knock off for work and head to bed.

Avoid alcohol if you need to get a good night's sleep. While alcohol is a depressant, you'll get less restful sleep when the effects on your central nervous system wear off.

Remember this guideline: Eat breakfast like a king, lunch like a prince and dinner like a pauper.

Try to eat at least three hours before going to sleep. Eat more non-starchy complex carbohydrates, whole grains and nuts, and less fat and protein. It's OK to eat some lean protein with your meal, but look for low-fat choices. Avoid sugar and caffeine. If you want dessert, stick with fruit, rather than baked goods or chocolate.

Drinks like warm milk and non-caffeinated peppermint herb tea may help you get to sleep by relaxing you, but don't affect your physiology, and therefore won't work like a drug to help you sleep. Add cocoa or chocolate to milk and you may have even more trouble falling to sleep because of the added caffeine, sugar and theobromine.

## Exercise and Sleep

Many of us have "slept like a baby" after playing tennis, volleyball, basketball, working hard in the yard, running or exercising.

While the jury is still out on the exact physiological reasons why exercise helps us sleep better, multiple studies on people suffering from insomnia have found that when they exercise, these people sleep better without medication.

What kind of exercise should you do to help yourself get a good night's sleep and when should you do it? Moderate intensity activity, such as aerobic exercise that makes you sweat, done five to six hours before you want to sleep, may be your best combination.

You may be surprised to hear aerobic exercise described as moderate intensity, but this differs from high-intensity exercise such as sprint training. Aerobic exercise uses your slow-twitch muscles fibers and is performed at a rate you can continue for long periods without having to stop.

Sprint training takes place at close to your maximum heart rate and you perform sprints in cycles of 30 to 90 seconds, using more high-twitch muscle fibers. Tennis is a good example of an anaerobic activity. Basketball, volleyball, football, racquetball and soccer are other examples. Very high intensity exercise can affect your dopamine levels, interfering with sleep.

In short, 30 minutes of moderately intense exercise stresses your muscles, increases your heart rate, raises your body's temperature, creates lactic acid in your muscles, produces more serotonin and depletes your stores of glycogen. It may be that your body's attempt to recover from this physical stress is what causes you to fall asleep more quickly and get a more deep, restful sleep.

One important aspect of this may be the temperature affect on your body. You may find it difficult to sleep if you go to shortly after exercise. This may be related to an elevated body temperature, in addition to your elevated heart rate and metabolism. If you exercise early, your body temperature, which began decreasing shortly after you stopped exercising, may be able to lower itself better near bedtime, helping you fall asleep quicker.

## Avoid Caffeine

Avoid caffeine, contained in such items as chocolate, tea, coffee and sodas. If you use caffeine to try and stay awake and alert while you're finishing a project, this can lead to restless sleep. Stay alert by getting up from your desk every 30 minutes or so and raising your heart rate. Walk up and down stairs or jog in place. Raise light levels in the room.

# Chapter Summary

•Sleep in a dark room

•Wake in a room with light

•Aim for 8 hours of sleep per day

•Take naps

•Regulate the room temperature

•Use a sleep mask

•Try white noise

•Wear socks to sleep

•Take a break before going to bed

•Exercise 5 to 6 hours before bedtime

•Avoid caffeine in the evening

•Eat light carbs is eating closer to bedtime

•Invest in the right mattress for you

•Buy the right pillow(s) for you

•Hydrate

•If you are giving a presentation that requires images to be projected  onto a screen, don't turn the lights out, or just dim the lights in the front of the room, directly above the screen.

# Chapter 2:
# Eating Habits

The main difference between eating for health and eating for productivity has more to do with when you eat than what you eat.

Eating for your health focuses on eating a reasonable number of calories and choosing foods that help you prevent diseases and conditions. Eating to improve your productivity as a businessperson should focus on how often and when you eat, not simply what and how much you eat.

You will follow most of the principles of healthy eating when you eat for peak performance, but you'll pay more attention to your eating regimen instead of just watching you calories and reducing fatty foods.

Even if you're in perfect shape and the perfect weight, what you eat and when you eat it is important if you want to perform at your peak each day.

Your eating habits determine whether you will be alert, sluggish, happy, irritable, focused or groggy. Food fuels your muscles and brain and affects the hormones that regulate bodily functions and emotions.

There is a food and mood connection that's directly tied to how your brain chemistry reacts to certain foods. What you eat affects the production of hormones and neurotransmitters such as serotonin, endorphins, epinephrine, dopamine and norepinephrine that raise and lower your metabolism and affect your brain function.

Carbohydrates, for example, help produce serotonin, which can make you feel relaxed and pleasant. Too many carbs can make you sleepy and sluggish, too few can make you tense, nervous and agitated. Chocolate releases endorphins, which are chemicals that block pain and stimulate pleasure. Some types of chocolate contain enough caffeine to stimulate or overstimulate you, depending on what else you've eaten that day.

The key to eating for your workday is to regulate the amount and types of food going into your body so you can keep your blood glucose and insulin levels steady and efficient. This means that you'll want to snack during the day, in addition to your regular meals.

## Eat More Often

Eat something for breakfast each morning. If you don't eat between dinner and lunch the next day, you'll go as long as 18 hours without fueling your body and brain.

How does your car perform after you haven't changed the oil after 10,000 miles? Your engine will have to try and function on the sludge that's left in your engine.

Wen you skip breakfast, you deprive your brain of the fuel it needs as you begin trying perform important intellectual tasks. Research shows that depriving yourself of food can decrease cognitive functions such as processing and understanding new information, memory, verbal skills and spatial and visual understanding.

Would you rather pay a lawyer $300 an hour to work on your important case who hadn't eaten in 18 hours, or one who had eaten a healthy breakfast and a healthy morning snack to keep fueled? Which one would be more likely to be alert, have better cognitive functions and less irritable, tense or sluggish?

If you were going in for open-heart surgery, would you want your doctor to operate on you if he had hadn't since the night before and had low blood insulin and glucose levels?

Then why would you ask to be paid full price by a client or employer and then work for them on an empty stomach?

If you're skipping breakfast to try and lose weight, you'll actually increase the likelihood you'll gain weight. You don't overeat when you're not hungry — you overeat when you're "starved." If you stuff yourself with excess calories, your body won't be able to metabolism them and will store them as fat.

Forget the big lunches and late dinners you think are buying you extra hours of work — they actually make you less productive, and you will likely only increase the quantity of lower-quality work you do.

## Suggested Eating Schedule

A good eating schedule for maintaining workplace productivity would look something like this:

7:00 am – Breakfast
10:00 am – Snack
12:00 pm – Lunch
3:00 pm – Snack
6:00 pm – Dinner

## What to Eat

Carbs are not the enemy. They never have been.

In fact, most of you daily calories should come from complex carbohydrates, whether you are eating for mental or physical performance or weight loss. Some reputable health organizations even recommend that protein make up a minority of your calories — about equal to or slightly less than the amount of fat you eat.

Yep. You can eat more fat than protein each day and still be healthy. How can this be?

Not all carbs, protein and fat are equal.

If you eat healthy fats, such as those found in plants and fish, you can eat more. Saturated and trans fats, found in large quantities in animal products and processed foods, such as baked goods, are the ones you want to avoid. Examples of food rich in healthy monounsaturated and polyunsaturated fat and omega-3 fatty acids include olive oil, peanut butter and salmon.

Cutting down on "bad" carbs or "white" carbs lets you eat more complex carbohydrates with more benefits. For example, instead of a white potato, eat a sweet potato. Instead of white bread, eat whole grain bread. Eat more veggies than pasta, rice and breads.

When you eat protein, choose lean sources. Coldwater fish, such as salmon and tuna, chicken and turkey breast meat, nuts, eggs, beans, peas and low-fat dairy products are good choices of lean protein.

At the end of this chapter is a list of healthy food choices for breakfast, lunch, dinner and snacks. You'll find a list of substitutes for some of your less-healthy favorites that still let you eat foods you like.

Aim for more than 50 percent of your daily calories from whole grains, nuts, legumes and seeds. Split the remaining calories between healthy fats and lean proteins.

## Snack Like You Mean It

The key to controlling calories and maintaining blood glucose levels is to eat at least two healthy snacks during the day. Your snacking needs to be proactive, not reactive. This means you need to plan your snacks each day, rather than simply heading to the vending machine each time you feel peckish.

Snacking for peak performance is not that difficult, even at work. You can keep a number of healthy snacks in your desk drawer, such as granola bars, oatmeal packets, microwave popcorn, trail mix, granola and nuts. If you work from home, keep your refrigerator stocked with sliced carrots and celery, fresh fruit and low-fat dips, such as hummus.

A quick, healthy snack at work might be as simple as a large handful of unsalted mixed nuts and a glass of water. A few celery sticks with 2 tbsp. of peanut butter is another good choice. You don't need to cook or fill yourself up with a large snack to regulate your glucose levels throughout the day.

Add protein to a snack to help stave off hunger pangs high-carb snacks can cause. A low-fat yogurt cup is a good snack after a carb-heavy meal.

Stay away from candy bars or sugary drinks. Sugar gives you a quick spike in your blood sugar levels, but will make you crash later. Oatmeal is a good source of complex carbs and is released into your system more evenly than a sugary snack.

## Healthy Snack Choices*

Granola bar
Piece of fruit
½ a bagel
Apples with peanut butter
Celery with peanut butter
Lightly salted popcorn
Trail mix
Handful of nuts and a glass of water
Yogurt cup
Packet of instant oatmeal
Celery, carrots, peppers with hummus dips
Handful of raisins
Energy bars

*Keep snacks around 100 to 200 calories.*
*Choose snacks lower in saturated and trans fats, sugar and sodium.*

# The Low-Carb Myth

Think of yourself as an automobile. You are made primarily of steel and use either gasoline or diesel as fuel. Just because you're made of steel doesn't mean you run on steel.

Now think of yourself as a human. Much of your body is made from protein, but you body runs on glycogen and fat. How much of each depends on whether you're doing aerobic or anaerobic activity. Just as you wouldn't stuff steel down your car's gas tank, you don't want to stuff your body with protein if you want to make yourself run. When you are at the office, you're in an anaerobic state, so your main fuel should be complex carbohydrates.

It took the mainstream media decades to finally understand the obvious fallacy of high-protein, low-carb diets, which credible dietitians knew to dismiss from the beginning of the fad. Because of the amount of advertising purchased by proponents of low-carb diets and fantastic claims made by these marketers, the media basically ignored the fact no research proved that low-carb diets reduced weight more than "mainstream" diets. The media also didn't look into the fact that these fad diets caused problems such as dehydration, kidney problems, lack of calcium and other issues.

In short, low-carb diets are a bit of a joke because their premise is that if you eat too many calories of a high-carbohydrate diet and don't exercise, you'll get fat.

Guess what? If you eat too many calories of a high-protein, low-carb diet and don't exercise, you'll get fat.

For peak performance, eat a diet that's 50 percent to 60 percent complex carbohydrates, with the rest of your calories split roughly evenly between healthy fats and lean protein.

# Create a Plate

A good guide to determining your daily mix of calories is to divide your meals into three areas on your plate. Half of your plate should contain non-starchy vegetables. One quarter of your plate should contain starchy carbs, and the last fourth of your plate should contain lean protein. You can add a serving a lean dairy and a serving of fruit to complete your nutrient needs. A good guide for protein servings is to keep meat, fish and poultry servings no larger than your fist.

# How Many Calories?

How many calories you should eat each day depends on your age, height, weight and activity levels. There are many free, online calorie calculators that will help you determine the right number for you.

One the following page is a chart that lists the U.S. Department of Agriculture daily calorie recommendations for an example woman who is 5'4" and 126 lbs., and an example man who is 5'10" and 154 lbs.

# USDA Daily Recommended Calories

**Girls & Women**

| Age | Sedentary | Moderately Active | Active |
|---|---|---|---|
| 2-3 | 1,000-1,200 | 1,000-1,400 | 1,000-1,400 |
| 4-8 | 1,200-1,400 | 1,400-1,600 | 1,400-1,800 |
| 9-13 | 1,400-1,600 | 1,600-2,000 | 1,800-2,200 |
| 14-18 | 1,800 | 2,000 | 2,400 |
| 19-30 | 1,800-2,000 | 2,000-2,200 | 2,400 |
| 31-50 | 1,800 | 2,000 | 2,200 |
| 51+ | 1,600 | 1,800 | 2,000-2,200 |

**Boys & Men**

| Age | Sedentary | Moderately Active | Active |
|---|---|---|---|
| 4-8 | 1,200-1,400 | 1,400-1,600 | 1,600-2,000 |
| 9-13 | 1,600-2,000 | 1,800-2,200 | 2,000-2,600 |
| 14-18 | 2,000-2,400 | 2,400-2,800 | 2,800-3,200 |
| 19-30 | 2,400-2,600 | 2,600-2,800 | 3,000 |
| 31-50 | 2,200-2,400 | 2,400-2,600 | 2,800-3,000 |
| 51+ | 2,000-2,200 | 2,200-2,400 | 2,400-2,800 |

*Height & Weight* - This chart uses an example woman who is 5'4" and 120 lbs., and an example man who is 5'10" and 154 lbs.

*Activity Level* - "Active" means your daily routine includes physical activity similar to walking more than 3 miles at 3 to 4 mph. "Moderately Active" means your daily routine includes activity similar to walking 1.5 to 3 miles at 3 to 4 mph. "Sedentary" means you do little physical activity other than the ordinary tasks associated with daily living.

# Drink Enough Water

Many people do not drink enough water each day, or, at the very least, experience periods of several hours when they're under-hydrated. People often confuse a lack of hydration with hunger, and so you may grab a snack when you're really just thirsty.

You may have heard that it's a good idea to drink eight glasses of water each day to stay adequately hydrated. This is false. While you do need sufficient water each day, you get most of the amount you need each day from the foods and drinks you take in

It's a good idea to let your thirst guide you as a way to maintain proper hydration. The next time you feel hungry between meals, ask yourself if you're really hungry or just need some water. Drinking an extra two or three glasses of water each day can't hurt you and may help you reduce unplanned snacking. If you are in a management position at your place of business, have a water dispenser installed in the office to help keep your workers adequately hydrated.

It's also a myth that you shouldn't drink water shortly before, during or after meals because it dilutes the enzymes responsible for digestion. This isn't true; water helps break down food and may make it easier to digest.

If you drink a glass of water before a meal, you may also eat fewer calories. Don't artificially decrease your calorie intake by filling yourself with water as a diet strategy — drink water before meals only as a way to help you refrain from <u>overeating</u>.

If drinking water before a meal helps prevent you from going back for seconds, that's a good strategy. If drinking more than one glass of water fills you to the point that you can get away with having an energy bar for lunch, that's not a good idea. Remember, water will not stay in your stomach, keeping you full, until your next meal. You'll pass that water and be hungry again soon, leading to poor snacking or a reliance on the dreaded "willpower" to ignore hunger pangs until your next meal.

Get in the habit of drinking two glasses of water each day (once in the morning and once in the afternoon) to stay sufficiently hydrated and to help reduce the number of excess calories you might otherwise eat throughout the day.

# Dining Out

Most businesspeople will not be able to avoid dining out. You may also feel it's necessary at times to stop at the drive-through of fast food restaurants and eat in the card to accommodate your busy schedule.

Just because you can't eat healthy doesn't mean you can't eat healthier.

For example, if you order a Burger King Whopper without the cheese and mayo, you'll reduce the fat by almost 50 percent, the cholesterol by more than 35 percent, and the calories by almost 30 percent, according to the nutrition information at Burger King's website.

Compare a serving of a Domino's pizza with sausage and pepperoni to a serving with mushrooms, onions and green peppers. The veggie pizza has approximately 35 percent less fat, 20 percent fewer calories, 50 percent of the cholesterol and 30 percent less sodium.

So, while a hamburger or pizza may not be anyone's definition of health food, a burger without the mayo and cheese and a veggie pizza are healthier fast-food options if you can't give up your favorites.

Keeping this type of food substitution in mind, you can begin to shift your eating to even healthier options without giving up comfort foods or subsisting on tofu and sprouts.

For example, skip the hamburger in spaghetti sauce and order tomato instead of Alfredo sauce. Order a vegetable soup instead of a cream-based one. Have a bean burrito with salsa and avocado instead of one with ground beef, cheese and sour cream.

You can also order dishes that aren't on the menu. Even during busy times, kitchens may at least modify menu items. For example, ask for crushed nuts or a sprinkle of sesame seeds on your salad instead of croutons. Ask to hold the mayo and cheese on a burger and for extra tomatoes and lettuce. When you order French onion soup, ask for no crouton or cheese. Skip the cheese and sour cream that comes with chili. Ask for salsa with a baked potato instead of sour cream, cheese and bacon. Try fajitas with back beans instead of steak or chicken.

Be realistic when you order off the menu. If you go to a chain restaurant and ask for Alfredo sauce made with skim milk, low-fat cheese, no butter and egg whites only, the kitchen most likely won't be able to do that, since they pre-make their Alfredo sauce and don't make it for each order.

Another thing to keep in mind is that many restaurants put all their orders into a computer — they may not be able to enter a completely new dish you order, even if the chef could make it. Ask for a simple substitution a busy chef can make when you consider your dining options.

## Eating Slower Reduces Calories

Have you ever eaten a plate of food, decided to go back for seconds, then been interrupted with a phone call or e-mail? Did you notice that after you hung up the phone or hit "send," you weren't hungry any more and didn't have that second helping?

One reason why people gain weight is because they overeat, based on how fast they eat. It takes approximately 15 minutes for the hormones that tell your brain your stomach is full to make it from your stomach to your brain.

This is why it's almost impossible to take only one plate at a buffet. You've finished your first plate, which may have included a large amount of calories, but you're still hungry, since you ate it in less than 15 minutes. You smell all this wonderful food sitting just a few feet away and go back for seconds.

Quite often, people who go to buffets can't finish the second plate of food they've eaten because their brain finally "catches up" to their stomach while they are eating that plate. Or, after you finish the second plate, you are extremely uncomfortable, or stuffed, all at once, with no warning.

If you work from home, you may eat a plate of food that has more than enough calories to satisfy you, but during those minutes of lag time between your stomach and brain talking to each other, you head back to the kitchen for seconds.

You might also eat a frozen dinner or small portion at lunch and feel less than satisfied at the table. Within 15 minutes at home, or by the time to get back to the office, you are often satiated without eating anything else.

Realizing that hunger pangs at the lunch or dinner table are only temporary and that you won't feel this hunger for long will help you reduce the temptation to have seconds or order dessert.

So, if you eat slower, your stomach will "catch up" to your brain, and you'll be less likely to have seconds. This doesn't necessarily mean chewing more or taking longer between forkfuls. Penn State researchers found that people who ate a bowl of soup to start their meal ended up eating 20 percent fewer calories each time.

## Ignore Mom

How many times did your mother tell you, "Don't eat that, you'll spoil your dinner!"? Ignore mom and help control your calories. If you are going out to eat with co-workers or clients, have a small snack before you leave the office. By the time you get to the restaurant, you will be less likely to be "starving" to the point you order an appetizer or want to super size your order.

Start with a cup of soup or side salad before you eat your main entrée and you'll be able to order less and still be full. In fact, you may be able to fill yourself with a cup of soup, small salad, piece of whole grain bread and glass of tea, juice or water.

If you're going to a business reception or cocktail party where hors d' oeuvre will be served, snack before you get their so you can control yourself once you get there. These functions often occur in the even before dinner, and if you haven't eaten since lunch, you may make these high-calorie, high-fat snacks your dinner. If you're going out to dinner after a reception, this can make things even worse.

## When to Eat Carbs, Proteins and Fats

You'll want to regulate your blood glucose throughout the day and maintain a good mix of carbohydrates, protein and fat.

As we mentioned earlier, having sugar will cause give you a temporary spike in energy, but will cause you to crash even lower than where you started when the sugar spike wears off.

Start your day with a breakfast that consists of roughly two-thirds complex carbohydrates and one-third lean protein. Your mid-morning snack, lunch and/or afternoon snack can include more protein if they come from lean sources, but should still be about 50/50 carbs and protein.

If you are going to eat one meal that is protein-heavy, such as one with fish, chicken or beef as the "main" dish, make that meal lunch. You'll have plenty of time to digest that meal before you go to bed in the evening.

If you want meat for dinner, add it to a stir-fry or pasta, rather than having a large piece of meat with several side dishes. The fat from your protein will get all over the rice, pasta or veggies, giving you that flavor you crave with every forkful, but with much less fat, cholesterol and calories.

Complex carbohydrates, as opposed to simple sugars, include foods such as vegetables, rice, pasta, potatoes and breads. Concentrate on whole grain pastas and breads, brown rice, sweet potatoes and other "non-white," "non-starchy" or low-glycemic carbs. In the appendix of this books is a list of healthy carb choices.

If you are eating later in the evening, eat more carbs and less protein to avoid eating that interferes with your sleep. Have more of your daily protein at lunch, such as fish or lean chicken, rather than trying to down a steak at night.

## Energy-Shot Drinks

One method of increasing energy currently popular among businesspeople is the so-called energy drink. These drinks claim to stimulate you in positive ways without the negative side effects of traditional stimulants. Some claim they do not affect your body, but only target your brain. Others promise that once your energy boost is over, you'll go back to your regular energy level and not suffer a post-drink crash, as you do with sugary drinks and candy bars.

Some of these energy drinks rely heavily on stimulants that will lead to a crash, depending on the amount of sugar in them. Even if you only drop from your temporary high back to your regular metabolic rate, as one of these drinks advertises, you might experience that as a crash.

If you want to try an energy boost drink, experiment with them on the weekend, not when you are under the gun and need energy during your workweek. Imagine what a worse predicament you'll be in if you rely on one of these shots to keep you going and it doesn't, or if you do crash at some point after taking it.

# Fast-Food Tips

•Hold the mayo and cheese on hamburgers and other sandwiches. Add more lettuce and tomatoes for extra moisture.

•Order grilled chicken sandwiches instead of fried.

•If you don't like diet soda, fill your cup with 50% diet, then 50% regular; you likely won't notice the difference. Start with a smaller mix, if you eventually want to get to 75%/25%.

•Skip the meat on pizza.

•Order thin crust pizza.

•Ask for less cheese on your pizza. Many pies come with a double layer.

•Order a bean burrito. Skip the sour cream and cheese and add salsa.

# Sit-Down Restaurant Tips

•Order a glass of water and drink at least half, even if you order soda.

•Start every meal with a cup (not a bowl) of low-fat soup or a salad. Skip the crackers and bread with it.

•Don't eat more than five chips if you get a basket of chips and salsa.

•Have a snack before you go to a sit-down restaurant. By the time you wait for friends, chat and order, you are likely to be very hungry and order more than you need.

•Order off the menu. Ask for simple substitutions to existing dishes, not for new items.

# Performer's Breakfast Items

**Oatmeal** – Add a dash of skim milk, a pat of butter substitute or a few raisins for added flavor.

**Cold cereal** – Some are made from nuts; choose those higher in complex carbs.

**Breads** – Choose whole grain toast, bagels and muffins and look for those with no trans fats.

**Yogurt** – Add protein to your carbs with a cup of low-fat yogurt. Mix in a pieces of fresh fruit for flavor or granola for crunch.

**Fruit** – Canned or fresh, fruit is a good source of vitamins and minerals and sweetens bland cereals, oatmeal, waffles and pancakes.

**Waffles and pancakes** – Choose whole grain versions and use a pat of non-fat butter substitute, a dash of syrup, a bit of yogurt or some fruit for extra flavor.

**Cottage cheese** – Use the fat-free variety as a small side dish and flavor it with fruit. This is a good source of protein and calcium.

**Turkey bacon** – If you need some meat, try a low-fat bacon made from turkey breast.

**Lean ham** – A good meat choice with pancakes and waffles.

**Egg whites and egg substitutes** – A healthy way to enjoy your eggs in the morning.

**Coffee cup "omelet"** – eliminate cholesterol in eggs by ditching the yokes. Make a quick soufflé with egg whites, veggies, lean ham and low-fat cheese. Put the mixture in a coffee cup and heat for 30 seconds. Stir the mixture and cook for another 30 seconds to your desired consistency.

# Performer's Healthy Lunch Items

*Low-fat soups* – Stay away from cream-based soups and look for vegetable varieties like tomato, onion, celery, black bean and vegetable.

*Salads* – Order dressing on the side and dip your fork in it before you spear your salad each time. Skip croutons or use baked, whole-grain croutons. Add nuts and seeds. Skip creamy dressing and cheese. Add a few spoonfuls of cottage cheese.

*Sandwiches* – Use whole grain bread. Skip mayo or use fat-free mayo or mustard. Use a small amount of lean meat to flavor sandwiches packed with lettuce, tomatoes, onions, sprouts, cucumbers, shaved carrots and avocadoes. Put the meat on the top so your first flavor is the meat. Use turkey and chicken breast and lean ham.

*Bean burrito* – Choose vegetarian or fat-free refried beans and add shredded lettuce, tomatoes, onions, avocado, salsa and low-fat sour cream. Serve with Spanish rice with diced red and green peppers.

*Tuna and chicken salad* – Use low-fat or fat-free mayo. Use chicken breast meat or water-packed, "light" canned tuna. Season with curry powder or tarragon. Add celery and onions, slivered almonds for crunch and grapes for sweetness.

*Ground turkey sliders* – If you haven't tried ground turkey burgers, you'll be hooked once you do. Order one or two sliders instead of a quarter pound beef burger to reduce calories, fat and cholesterol. Pile on the lettuce, tomato and onions. Serve with a side like baked sweet potato fries, low-fat potato salad or baked beans.

# Performer's Healthy Dinner Items

*Pasta* – Choose whole-grain pasta and serve and don't drown it in sauce. Choose tomato sauce or toss it lightly in olive oil and garlic. Flavor with shrimp, chicken breast strips or canned tuna.

*Salmon* – Bake, poach, grill or broil. Season with black pepper or garam masala. Bake or broil over asparagus spears, mushrooms and thin slices of potato.

*Pizza* – Choose a whole-grain, thin crust. Top with half the normal amount of cheese. Add your favorite veggies.

*Chicken breast* – Grill, bake or broil. Season lightly with salt and pepper, tarragon or garam masala. Serve with a half a sweet potato and mixed vegetables.

*Beef* – The closer you are to bedtime, the less beef you should eat. Choose leaner cuts of beef, such as sirloin or flank. They're less expensive and have less cholesterol and fat. Use beef to flavor stir-fry dishes, rather than having a large piece of meat with several side dishes. Serve with baked beans and fresh vegetables.

*Mac and cheese* – Use whole-grain pasta, low-fat cheese and skim milk for this dish. Skip the eggs, butter and full cheese and add tarragon to your low-fat cheese sauce for an upscale, grownup comfort food. Add sliced cherry tomatoes and a small amount of lean ham cubes. Add sliced onions or mushrooms for a more savory flavor. Serve with a salad and fat-free dressing.

*Breakfast for Dinner* – No one says you can't have a couple of pancakes or waffles and a slice of lean ham for dinner. Serve with a pat of non-fat butter substitute, a dash of syrup and fresh fruit. Avoid orange, grapefruit or tomato juice if the acid will keep you awake later.

# Chapter Summary

• East breakfast (2/3 carbs, 1/3 protein).

• Eat at least five times each day (three meals each day and two snacks).

• Keep meals around 400-600 calories and snacks to 100-200 calories.

• Create a Plate (½ non-starchy vegetables, ¼ protein, ¼ starchy vegetables).

• Keep protein (meat, fish, poultry, etc.) portions the size of your fist.

• Eat in courses (start with soup).

• Drink a glass of water each morning and afternoon.

• Substitute ingredients when dining out.

• "Spoil" your meal before dining out.

• Eat slower.

• Eat more protein earlier in the day and less later.

• Avoid energy drinks.

# Chapter 3:
# Raising Your Metabolism

You will improve your productivity if you are able to get more oxygen to your brain during the day, maintain a healthy resting heart rate, have good blood circulation, release chemicals that improve your mood and generally keep your metabolism up during the day.

You don't need to lift weights, go jogging, work out in a gym or use an exercise machine to stay fit for work — you can maintain an adequate metabolism level for good workplace productivity with a few simple techniques in your office and around the workplace.

Yes, vigorous exercise is extremely helpful for long-term weight loss and general health, but if you aren't interested in or can't commit to a regular exercise program, you can still perform a variety of simple activities each day that will raise your metabolism throughout your workday, improving your brain function — all without causing you to break a sweat.

Even if you are into exercise and are in great shape, your metabolism can still go down to unproductive levels during the day and you should try to get physical in and around the office to increase your heart rate, blood circulation and metabolism during working hours.

Sitting at your desk from 8:00 am and not moving until lunch is not a good idea. Raising your heart rate every 30, 60 or 90 minutes will help you perform better because of the increased oxygen flow to your brain and blood circulation throughout your body.

Taking a few minutes to raise your metabolism will prevent your heart rate from settling into an unproductive number of beats per minute. Just as raising your heart rate too high is bad for your health, letting your heart rate drop very low and stay there is bad for your productivity.

Getting up from your desk, walking around the office, doing a few quick exercises or walking up and down a flight of stairs or two is all you need to raise your metabolism for improved productivity. And you don't need to break a sweat.

## Stairs

How hard is it to walk up one or two flights of stairs? Not very difficult, but stairs are an excellent tool for breaks. Here's a good pattern for using stairs to raise your metabolism each day:

•Get off the elevator two flights early when you come to work in the morning, and walk the last two flights to your floor.

•After you have been at your desk for 90 minutes or more, leave your office and walk up and down two flights of stairs. You can also do  this after your mid-morning snack break.

•When you leave for lunch, take two flights of stairs down and get on the elevator on another floor.

•Get off the elevator two flights early when you return from lunch.

•Walk up and down two flights of stairs at least once during the afternoon.

•When you leave work, get off the elevator two floors early, or take the stairs down two floors before you get on the elevator.

This simple pattern will result in your walking up and down 16 flights of stairs each day, 80 flights each week, and 320 to 400 flights of stairs each month. During a 50-week work year, you'll walk 4,000 flights of stairs.

When you walk up stairs, you use more calf muscle to lift your body's weight and propel you upward. When you walk down stairs, you engage the quads more to brake you, varying your muscle use.

Depending on your office or your physical condition, you may only need to walk up and down one flight of stairs to get a quick heart rate increase, or you may need to walk more than two flights.

Using stairs to elevate your heart rate, improve your circulation and get more oxygen to your brain is a simple, effective way to increase your productivity on the job.

## Desk Exercises

Performing two or more minutes of simple movements in your chair or in front of your desk will help you get a quick burst of energy and raise your metabolism.

*Hip and Butt Raises* - Place your feet together in front of you. Place your hands on your chair near your hips. Raise your self slightly off your chair (you don't need to stand up straight) and lower yourself, repeating this exercise for 30 to 60 seconds.

Try this same exercise with your legs off the floor, straight in front of you. Use se your arms to raise your butt slightly off the chair.

*Desk Pushups* - Stand in front of your desk and lean forward, placing your hands on your desk. Use your arms to raise and lower yourself, performing these pushups for 30 to 60 seconds.

*Ups and Downs* - Stand in front of your desk with your feet about shoulder width and your hands on your hips. Bend forward and touch your hands to your knees, then touch your toes. Raise up and put your hands back on your hips, then reach as high toward the ceiling as possible. Continue this pattern for 30 to 60 seconds.

# More Serious Exercise

If you would like to improve your heart health, lose some weight, improve your sleep, better deal with stress and help avoid diseases and conditions such as high blood pressure, heart attack and stroke, you don't have to perform grueling, stressing, boring or unenjoyable workouts that cause you pain and leave you stiff and sore the next day.

The key to starting an exercise program is finding an activity or activities you enjoy doing. Choosing a piece of exercise equipment or signing up for a gym membership only because you know that it will be effective in getting you in shape or helping you lose weight is not a smart idea. If you don't look forward to your fitness activity, you'll start skipping workouts and eventually may quit altogether.

Enjoyment (fun!) should be your number one priority when choosing a long-term exercise activity if you want to stick with it. You can turn almost any physical activity into exercise with a few modifications to what you're doing, so think about enjoyable physical activities as you begin your planning.

If you like to play tennis or racquetball, schedule time for those and stick to your playing schedule. If you prefer to work out alone, don't sign up for an exercise class, no matter how good you've heard it is. If you are more social, sign up for a gym membership. If you hate jogging because of the leg and back pain it causes, but don't mind walking, choose that activity.

# Exercise Choices

There is no one type of exercise or workout that is best for everyone. You can get the benefits you want by performing a variety of exercises and workout routines, and may even want to cross train with several activities, rather than sticking with one workout each time.

Depending on your goals, you have the following options:

### Resistance Exercises

Resistance exercise focuses on building muscle. You use weights, resistance bands, exercise machines or bodyweight exercises to slightly damage your muscle fibers. When your muscles recover and repair themselves, they grow larger.

While you may not be interested in bodybuilding, using some resistance during exercise, including beginner and cardio workouts, can help you increase your calorie burn throughout the day and improve your fitness levels.

Working your core and lower back muscles, for example, can help reduce back pain. American workers lose more than 100 million workdays each year due to lower back pain, according to the Wellness Council of America. Larger muscles also burn more calories while you're sitting at your desk or going about your normal daily activities.

### Fat-Burning Workouts

Fat-burning is not a scientific term for workouts and generally refers to exercise done at a pace comparable to a brisk walk. When you exercise below your aerobic heart rate, you burn a higher percentage of calories from fat than from glycogen, which is why some people refer to this as fat-burning exercise. You'll actually burn less fat doing this type of exercise because you burn fewer total fat calories as compared to an aerobic workout. Fat-burning exercise still burns calories and is an excellent way to start building the stamina and endurance you'll need for more intense exercise.

### Aerobic Exercise

Aerobic exercise is activity you perform at a heart rate similar to the one you reach when jogging. You should be breathing hard, sweating, but still able to talk. If you can't talk, you're exercising in the anaerobic heart rate range, and may soon fatigue and have to stop.

You can use a heart rate monitor to gauge your aerobic target heart rate, which is 70 percent to 80 percent of your maximum heart rate, but heart rate formulas are often inaccurate. Some heart rate formulas and monitors you wear or that come with machines provide you with a good general guide for your workout intensity; however, you can follow your body's own feelings to achieve the best heart rate for exercise. The key is to find the maximum pace you can continually maintain for 15 minutes or longer without having to take frequent breaks.

### *Sprint/Interval Training*

Working at a high intensity for a very short period of time (less than two minutes), recovering, then starting again is called sprint or interval training. You can do this a variety of ways using weights, an exercise machine or with calisthenics or bodyweight exercises.

This type of training occurs at 80 percent to 90 percent of your maximum heart rate, or near your maximum effort. Without a heart rate monitor, you should aim for an intensity that almost exhausts you after 30 to 90 seconds. You then take a 15- to 30-second recovery break, then perform another sprint.

One method of exercising this way is with circuit training. Circuit training is a method of exercise that moves you from exercise to exercise, performing each one at a high intensity for a very short period of time to raise your hear rate.

For example, if you lift weights to build muscles, like a bodybuilder, you lift the maximum weight you can lift, or close to it. You perform only three to five lifts per set, taking a break after each set. With circuit training, you perform an exercise using about 50 to 75 percent of your maximum weight or effort for 30 to 60 seconds, depending on what shape you're in. You take only a 15- to 30-second break, then move to a new exercise. You might take a break of several minutes every 10 minutes, but your goal is to keep your heart rate high during the entire course of your workout.

You can use single- or multiple-exercise circuits. For a single-exercise circuit-training workout, you might perform jumping jacks for one minute, take a short break, then move to biceps curls, then do crunches and so on. With a multiple-exercise circuit-training workout, you might do 30 seconds of running in place, immediately move to 30 seconds of situps without a break, then move to another exercise, completing four, 30-second exercises before taking a one-minute break.

It's important to consult with a fitness professional or your doctor before you try this type of exercise. Even adding a few sprints to aerobic workouts should be OK'd by your doctor before you try this.

## Other Benefits of Exercise

Exercise provides a wide variety of health and fitness benefits that can keep you on the job and decrease tardiness, absenteeism and sick days. This, in turn, reduces health care costs and increases productivity. Benefits of exercise include:

•Reduced lower back pain
•Improved heart health
•Weight loss and maintenance
•Reduced stress
•Improved blood cholesterol
•Reduced risk of heart attack and stroke
•Improved mental acuity
•Improved sleep

## Creating a Home Workout Area

If you can dedicate an area in your home for exercise, you'll be more likely to exercise on a regular basis. If you have to drag out a machine or find and set up other equipment, you may skip your workout.

It's easy to create a workout space or room in your home with items you have around the house. If you're more motivated, you can outfit your exercise area with variety of low-cost cardio and resistance equipment.

To begin, find a space in your home you can use each time you want to work out. If you need to use the room or space for other work, you'll just need a small container for any items you want to keep in the room.

Make sure the room is well ventilated, well lit and preferably has a ceiling height that will let you raise your arms and jump slightly. The floor should be level and firm, but not hard. If you have a wood, tile or concrete floor, buy an exercise mat.

Have a table for your cell phone, water bottle, glasses, towel or other items. If you plan on keeping items like resistance bands, a jump rope, dumbbells or an ab wheel in the room, keep a box in the room.

Add some creature comforts, such as a TV you can watch during workouts to make them go faster. If you have a DVD player, you can follow along with workout programs. Leave a radio, iPod or other player in the room if you enjoy music or want to listen to an audio book.

Include some or all of these items to help you work out:

•Dumbbells
•Resistance bands
•Gym ball
•Kettlebell
•Ab wheel
•Jump rope
•Hula hoop
•Plastic milk jugs/soda bottles (water-filled weights)
•Bike trainer/stand
•Chin-up bar
•Two, stable chairs (for dips)
•Heart rate monitor

# About Exercise Equipment

## *Dumbbells*

If you want to build some muscle to help improve your ability to burn more calories throughout the day and perform better physically, consider dumbbells. You can buy dumbbells cheaply at most local sporting goods stores. You do not need a dumbbell set, and may be able to get away with only one. Dumbbells are an excellent choice for circuit-training workouts.

Women should choose a weight of 2.5 pounds to 10 pounds, depending on whether you will be using them during aerobic workouts or using them during a portion of some workouts. Men should start with 10-pound dumbbells or higher for cardio workouts, and heavier weights for bodybuilding. The key is to choose a weight you can continue to use without having to stop your workout after only a few minutes. As you build your strength, you can buy heavier dumbbells.

## *Kettlebells*

A kettlebell looks like a bowling ball with a handle. You can use a kettlebell in much the same way you use dumbbells. The handle makes the kettlebell unstable, since the weight does not have a uniform shape. This requires you to recruit your core muscles during exercises to keep yourself balanced, adding another benefit to your exercises. To choose the right weight kettlebell, determine if you can use the weight for 15 minutes or more without having to stop your workout due to sore muscles.

An excellent way to build muscle, burn calories and improve your core all at once is with kettlebell swinging. Start with the kettlebell on the floor in front of you, between your legs, which should be about shoulder width apart. Squat down, sticking your buttocks backward, lowering yourself while you keep your torso straight and your eyes straight ahead. Grasp the kettlebell with one or two hands, depending on the weight you are using. Swing the kettlebell straight up to shoulder or head height, using a simultaneous upward leg drive and forward hip thrust. Let the ball fall back down between your legs, keeping it off the floor as you swing it up and down over and over again.

Make sure you keep a straight torso and use your legs, hips and arms — not your back — do swing the kettlebell. You can take frequent breaks during kettlebell swinging as long as you keep them short and keep your heart rate elevated throughout the workout.

### Home Gyms and Weight Machines

You can use home gyms and weight machines with low resistance settings to create cardio and weight-loss workouts. While you may think of these machines as bodybuilding tools, if you use very little weight while performing the exercises, you can raise your heart rate for longer periods while you work your muscles. The key is to find a weight or resistance setting for each exercise that doesn't fatigue you to failure. Use this type of gym equipment to create cardio and circuit-training workouts.

### Cardio Machines

Cardio machines include such equipment as treadmills, ellipticals, rowers, Gazelles, exercise bikes and other machines that let you exercise at your aerobic heart rate for many minutes. They can be extremely beneficial for beginners, intermediates or advanced exercisers. They can also be expensive, boring, limiting and cause repetitive stress injuries.

Even if you find an exercise machine you like using and will continue to use, you'll limit the benefit of exercise you get over time as your body adapts to the limited muscles you use on one machine. You can also cause bodily stress by working the same muscles, tendons and ligaments the same way over and over. It's best to use a variety of cardio machines, switching which machine you use each workout, or moving from machine to machine every 10 minutes during a workout. If you want to buy a cardio machine for your home or office, use it in conjunction with other workout methods, such as calisthenics or circuit-training with dumbbells or resistance bands.

## Target Heart Rates

Your target heart rate range is the number of heartbeats per minute you want to achieve during exercise. You don't need to hit one number, but instead want to be in a range that lets you know whether you are in your fat-burning, aerobic or anaerobic heart rate range.

You target heart rate range for each level of exercise is a percentage of your maximum heart rate, or how many beats your heart can make in one minute.

For beginners, your fat-burning heart rate range is roughly 50 percent to 60 percent of your maximum heart rate. Aerobic exercise takes place at 70 percent to 80 percent of your maximum heart rate. Sprint training takes place at 80 percent to 90 percent of your maximum heart rate.

To calculate your maximum heart rate, you can take a treadmill stress test, administered by a health professional, input data into a heart rate monitor, or use a manual calculation.

For many years, people used the formula 220 – Your Age to get their maximum heart rate. This was never intended by the two physicians who offered it as a general example, but the public soon began to misquote this formula as the Holy Grail for determining maximum heart rate. Today, credible exercise physiologists do not use this formula, though it is still the most commonly cited among the general population.

There is no universally accepted formula for manually calculating maximum heart rate, but Northwestern Memorial Hospital researchers determined that adult women should subtract 88 percent of their age from 206 to get the most accurate maximum heart rate. Of the many other formulas available, most will give you a maximum heart rate within two or three beats of each other.

Using the Northwestern formula, a 30-year-old formula would multiply 30 X .88 to get 26.4. She would subtract that from 206 to get 179.6. To get her target heart rate range for exercise, she would multiply 179.6 by .70 and .80 to get a target heart rate range for aerobic exercise of roughly 126 to 144 beats per minute. Using the old 220 – Age formula, she would have tried to maintain a target heart rate range of 133 to 152 beats per minute.

The most accurate way to determine your maximum heart rate is with a stress test, with a health professional taking into account your gender, weight, age, resting heart rate and other personal factors.

For most people, you can estimate your target heart rate for exercise as follows:

***Beginner/Fat-burning*** – Similar to a heart rate attained during a brisk walk. You should be breathing harder, but not sweating profusely.

***Intermediate/Aerobic*** – Similar to jogging. You should be breathing hard and sweating, but able to talk. You should be able to continue for 15, 30 or 60 minutes at this pace.

*Advanced/Anaerobic* – Similar to fast running, but not flat-out sprinting. You will tired after 30 to 120 seconds and need to stop.

## Heart Rate Monitors

A heart rate monitor is a helpful tool you can use while you work, as well as when you exercise. At least twice a month at work, wear your heart rate monitor during quiet, morning hours and note your resting heart rate. Check your heart rate after you have been sitting calmly for 15 minutes or more. Check it again a while later. Write down your heart rate each time to track your resting heart rate. You should not have any caffeine or sugar, be under deadline stress, have just walked up stairs or performed other physical activity.

After you know your resting heart rate, check it again after you take a two- or three-minute exercise break, such as desk exercises or walking stairs. Use your heart rate to alert you to a very low physical state or agitated one. If you need to make a tough phone call or difficult presentation, check your heart rate. If it's too rapid, try to lower it with deep breathing.

A healthy resting heart rate for most people is anywhere from 60 to 100 beats per minute, depending on how well conditioned you are. The lower your resting heart rate, the better cardiovascular shape you're in. As you exercise, you resting heart rate might decrease. Make sure to adjust your exercising target heart rate range as you improve.

## Treadmill Tests

To get an accurate assessment of your heart health, treat yourself to a stress test, often performed on a treadmill. Qualified professionals will assess your cardiopulmonary capacity and stamina and let you know your resting and maximum heart rate, giving you target heart rate ranges for beginner, intermediate and advanced workouts. In addition to evaluating you for exercise, your health professional can determine whether you have an abnormal heart rhythm or have other warning signs of poor heart health.

# Chapter Summary

• Boosting your metabolism helps your brain function better.

• Get up from your desk for a minute or two each hour.

• Walk stairs each day.

• Learn two or three easy desk exercise to do every hour or so.

• Workout at any pace you can sustain for 30 minutes or more without pain.

• Choose exercise you enjoy doing, rather than "the best" workout.

• Add some resistance to workouts.

• Invest in a heart rate monitor – some reliable ones cost as little as $30.

• Take a treadmill stress test.

• Create a simple workout area in your home.

• Add a fitness wellness component to your workplace to reduce absenteeism and healthcare costs and to increase productivity.

# Chapter 4:
# Reducing Stress

Have you ever been driving in your car, then suddenly, a police car turned on its lights behind you? Your first reaction may have been a sudden and slight case of panic. "What did I do?," "What's happening?," "Am I going to get a ticket?"

Your heart rate probably went up. Your hands may have started to shake a bit. Your mouth might have gone dry.

Why did you suddenly have these physical reactions to your thoughts? No one had touched you. Your car was not out of control. You were not in any immediate danger . . . yet you manifested physical reactions to the thought of being pulled over.

If the police officer ended up not pulling you over and sped around you to go on another call, your heart rate then went down, your muscles relaxed and you started breathing deeper.

Do you know why these physical responses happened?

Based on what you are thinking, you brain releases different chemicals which affect your central nervous system. These hormones and neurotransmitters can make you feel relaxed, tense, excited, nervous, motivated or scared.

If you're stressed, you may experience high levels of epinephrine. If you're in a good mood, you can probably thank dopamine. If you're sleepy, you have elevated levels of melatonin. Elevated serotonin levels can lead relaxation, while too little can lead to anger or depression.

When you are stressing, your brain will release adrenaline and/or noradrenaline (also known as epinephrine and norepinephrine), which affect your nervous system. Physical reactions to the release of these chemicals include an elevated heart rate, a spike in blood pressure, sweating, shortness of breath, lack of saliva production and jittery muscles.

A sudden release of adrenaline creates the "fight or flight" syndrome, which is that feeling you experience that causes you to consider reacting to a situation offensively or defensively.

Depending on what is occurring during your workday, your brain will release stimulate chemical production based on what it thinks you need to cope with the situation. This can have positive or negative affects. For example, if you have to give a speech in front of a roomful of people and you are not comfortable doing that, you can start to perspire, shake, get dry mouth, stammer or feel light headed or dizzy. If you love making sales presentations, your heart rate will rise, you'll feel positive and you'll have extra energy.

Many common situations can cause your brain to release stress hormones, including:

- Having to confront, discipline or terminate an employee
- Making a sales call (in person or on the phone)
- Dealing with an irate client or customer
- Public speaking
- Being interviewed by the media
- Facing a deadline
- Dealing with a financial crisis
- Asking for a raise
- Being called into your superior's office for a reprimand

Stressful situations cause short-term physical reactions, while prolonged stress and the release of stress hormones and neurotransmitters over and over again can suppress your immune system, making you more susceptible to colds, flus and other ailments.

One example of stress causing illness is the story of a successful six-sigma black belt project consultant who was under such pressure during one client engagement, her stomach began releasing excess acid, damaging her vocal chords to the point she lost her voice before the project was over. Her subordinate had to deliver her final presentation. Another example includes a teenage ice skater who was under such stress from her parents to win, she had to withdraw from multiple tournaments because she became ill with a cold or flu and had to stay home in bed.

Reducing stress is critical to achieving not only situational peak performance, but also long-term health and productivity. How can you deal with stressful situations that affect you physically?

## Identify Stressful Situations

Don't wait until you face stressful situations to try and respond to them. Write a list of situations you feel cause you to stress. These could include regular occurrences, such as sales calls, employee reviews, deadlines or public speaking.

If you can identify stressful situations you experience, you can create ways to minimize, avoid or deal with them. Dealing with stress successfully requires a proactive, not reactive process.

Stress me once, shame on you. Stress me over and over again, shame on me. Don't accept the fact that certain situations stress you out and that they are just part of doing business. Even if you can't eliminate them, you can minimize their impact on your performance, productivity and long-term health.

## Prepare/Rehearse

Decide if you can identify when stressful situations you have identified will occur before they occur. This will help you learn to identify stressful situations as soon as they begin to happen.

Being able to identify and recognize stressful situations will help you prepare for them in advance. When stress starts to occur, you can then have a plan in place to immediately and successfully cope with it.

Once you have identified stressful situations, develop ways to deal with them and practice these techniques in advance. These techniques can be as simple as controlling your breathing.

Controlling your breathing can help lower your heart rate. Take a deep breath and hold it for two or three seconds. Slowly let it out. You should feel a release of the physical tension in your shoulders and a decreased heart rate. Try this now.

Breathe through your nose to pull deeper breaths into your lungs. Try this now.

Another technique you can use to combat stress caused by another person is to pause before you verbally respond. Count to two before you answer a question, accusation or other stressful verbal communication. This will help you become proactive as you answer, rather than reactive.

Practice receiving a question or comment, then mentally counting to two before you answer, even if you know the answer you want to give. You might tap your finger against your thigh twice, lick your lips or just mentally count, "One thousand, two thousand," before you answer.

Another technique to help reduce the effects of stress is to avoid sugar and caffeine if you are going into a stressful situation. Eat more complex carbohydrates, which helps with serotonin production, which can help relax you. If you can visit a humorous website, watch a comedy clip. Laughter requires more oxygen, which has a therapeutic effect on your body, and deep laughter can stimulate serotonin production in your muscles.

When you're nervous, you may avoid eye contact. Your employee, client or prospective customer may notice your eyes darting up and down and around the room. If you can't look someone in the eye when you are under stress, focus on their nose or lips to keep your eyes centered. If you can make eye contact, be aware of your nerves and make sure you maintain your eye contact.

Practice the following techniques to respond to stressful, person-to-person situations:

•Place your hands on your hips as a positive show of confidence.
•Look into the other person's eyes.
•Uncross your arms and legs, if you have crossed them.
•Sit or stand up straight.
•Pause for two seconds before responding verbally — don't talk over someone. You will seem in better control.

## Recognize and React

Are you a pushover? Can employees come in late without penalty? Do you accede to deadline extension requests, or allow missed deadlines without consequences?

When you cave in because you are too afraid to hurt someone's feelings or can't deal with conflict or confrontation, you can carry your embarrassment, frustration or other negative feelings with you. You can lose self-confidence or self-esteem, which will continue to nag at you. You can carry anger toward a particular co-worker, supplier, vendor, client or your employer.

Learn to deal with conflict, which can be as easy as saying, "No" or giving a subordinate or co-worker an option that contains a carrot and stick to change behavior. For example you can extend a deadline, but the employee will need to stay late to finish the job. If you give a deadline, assume it won't be met and be prepared with a response.

You can also try to avoid stress. Don't wait for bad news. If you have assigned deadlines, check in with your client, vendor or employee shortly before the deadline to get a report on their status. Ask if they will make their deadline, if they are facing any problems and if they need any help from you.

Quite often, someone who misses a deadline knows in advance they won't make the deadline. Instead of alerting the proper people, they wait until deadline to inform you of the situation. Let people you give deadlines to know they need to let you know as soon as possible if they might miss the deadline. Set a date to check in with them or assign status reports.

Read your list of potentially stressful situations and learn to recognize when they might occur. Learn to implement the stress-reducing techniques you've practiced as soon as you recognize stressful situations.

Many responses to stress can make you look weak or guilty, even if you are not. Simple body language you may not notice include things such as crossing your arms and legs, mumbling, slouching, avoiding eye contact, putting your hands in your pockets or tugging on a piece of clothing or jewelry. More obvious responses include stammering and sweating.

For many bullies, the best defense (when they are wrong) is a strong offense. Learn to recognize when you are on the defensive and use body language and other techniques to get into a controlled state; now, you can become offensive.

For example, your first reaction to a confrontation might be to take a deep breath, let it out, then pause before you answer. Once you have controlled yourself, uncross your legs, place both feet on the floor and sit up straight if you are sitting. If you're standing, uncross your arms and place your hands on your hips. Look the other person in the eyes. Be careful that you don't present a combative body language, such as leaning into someone, moving into their personal space or pointing your finger at them. Find the right balance of confidence and control to let the other person know you are not afraid of them, and that they are not "winning."

Understand that there are times you want to project a neutral stance, especially with a client or superior. You don't want to be defensive, but you don't want to be antagonistic. You want to project an image that there is no stress in the room, and that there's no problem. You are oblivious to any negativity. If they see you are relaxed, this can let the other person relax. They might rethink their perception of the situation if you are not negative about it.

Sitting slouched, with your arms crossed, sends a negative, defensive message. Sitting up straight, making eye contact, speaking in a loud voice and leaning forward can send an offensive message. Leaning back in your chair with your hands on your thighs can send a relaxed, neutral message.

Remember, no one can cause you stress — but you can <u>let</u> them cause you stress. If you think a situation is stressful, then it is. If you decide that you are not defensive, you will be offensive.

## Dealing with Ongoing Stress

If you have a stressful job, the long-term physical effects can become serious. You can develop an ulcer, high blood pressure, sleep and digestive problems and a suppressed immune system. These can lead to depression, anxiety, anger, lack of focus and eventually increase your risk of heart attack and stroke.

Some self-help gurus suggest you learn techniques to avoid or minimize stress. Other experts suggest you subject yourself to controlled stress, such as competitive sports or rigorous exercise, to learn to handle more stress.

If you are under stress for long periods of time, you'll need more than just on-the-job techniques to deal with them.

Adequate sleep and exercise are two key factors in addressing stress. As the chapter of this book on sleep revealed, sleep helps repair cell damage and provides other physical and mental benefits that can help you reduce the effects of sleep.

# Sports = Controlled Stress

Your thoughts affect not only your physiology, but also your actions. You often make bad decisions under stress.

Consider the tennis player who is facing set point and misses her first serve. What is her response to this pressure? In many cases, she will double fault, and if so, she will probably hit her serve into the net, rather than long or wide. Why?

Because tennis players toss their balls lower when they are trailing Love-40 or 15-40 than when they are leading 40-love or 40-15.

Why do tennis players this? Because a high toss requires you to reach higher and get on your toes or off your feet to go after the ball. When tennis players are nervous, they keep the ball close to their bodies and stay on their heels so they can control the ball better. They don't go for it . . . because they are under stress.

So, the thought of being down set point and having a second serve creates mental stress. This mental stress results in physiological reactions, such as a higher heart rate and weak muscles. This physical reaction to stress causes you to make bad decisions (a low toss), and leads to failure (double fault).

Sports repeatedly puts you under <u>controlled</u> stress (double faulting or missing a putt won't cost your company thousands or millions of dollars). It teaches you to recognize stress. It shows you what your reactions to stress are. And it repeatedly gives you the opportunity to practice addressing your stress and using techniques to minimize it.

Well-coached tennis players recognize a high-pressure serving situation. They take something off the serve and get a first serve in, rather than taking a chance on facing the stress of a second serve. They toss their balls higher and decide that if they are going to miss, they are going to miss with confidence, not out of fear. They learn to take a deep breath, hold it, and release it slowly to lower their heart rate.

Playing sports helps you learn to experience, recognize, control and overcome stress.

An old tennis maxim states, "If you're going to double fault, double fault long." This is a method top players have for dealing with the stress of a second serve. They force themselves to toss the ball high, just as they would when they are winning and feeling positive.

In addition to reducing or avoiding stress in your life, you should learn how to handle stress, and more of it. Sports allows you to voluntary experience stress in a controlled environment without the pressure of the many negatives associated with business stress.

For example, the score in a sports game or match puts stress on you. Targets, such as goals, boundaries, receivers and holes put stress on you. Outcomes, such winning or breaking 100 during a golf game put stress on you.

These are examples of stresses that challenge your mind and body in positive ways. The most mentally tough competitors, in sports or business, love challenges and pressure. Participating in sports helps you expose yourself to pressure, learn to deal with it, learn not to fear it and learn techniques for overcoming it.

What is "first hole jitters" in golf? It's the nervousness many golfers feel when they hit their first shot of the day. Why would your first drive cause you to be more nervous than any other shot during your round? Because you want to start well and not make a fool of yourself in front of your associates or friends. Your fellow players are watching you to see how their afternoon with you is going to go. If you top the first ball or slice it way into the woods, you know they will be thinking, "Oh great! I'm stuck with this hack all afternoon."

Even though you use the same swing to hit your first tee shot that you'll be using over and over the next 17 holes, you are still nervous. But it's only because you put this pressure on yourself. This is an excellent example of facing stress in a controlled situation and learning how to overcome it.

Participating in sports, as simple as playing golf, racquetball, tennis or three-on-three basketball, provides you the important benefit of being able to repeatedly expose yourself to stress in controlled situations so you can learn to overcome it.

## Traffic and Stress

Traffic can cause you significant stress each day, making you arrive at the office in a tense, bad mood. It can also maintain or raise your stress levels after work, making you nervous and irritable when you get home.

Think about why you get upset in traffic. In the morning, does traffic make you late for work? At night, does someone cutting you off or driving slowly make you lean on the horn?

Traffic and bad drivers can't stress you out. You can <u>let</u> them stress you out, but if you learn to accept the inevitable situations that arise in traffic over and over again, realize that bad traffic won't kill you and refuse to let other drivers or slow traffic drive you crazy, you can eliminate significant stress in your life each day.

If you are in management, consider de-stressing your employees by offering parking options that let them park close to your building in a safe, easy-access environment. Offer to buy rail or bus passes, set up a carpool van or give employees who carpool free and covered parking.

# Exercise

Exercise helps you deal with stress differently than playing sports does. Exercise burns energy, raises your heart rate and releases brain hormones that can elevate your mood. Unlike sports, exercise has none of the scoring, target or other performance pressure that can negatively affect your mood.

This is why, unlike athletes during games and matches, joggers and weightlifters rarely throw their equipment around and smash things while working out.

Exercise also helps you sleep better, a key tool in the fight against stress.

If you are in a position to add a wellness program to your workplace, help your workers reduce stress by offering free or reduced-priced gym memberships, personal trainer consultations or lectures, weight-loss contests, rebates on exercise equipment or an on-site fitness room.

# Get Support

Don't try to deal with a high-pressure job or long-term negative situation by yourself. Even if you simply talk about your problems and vent to a family member or friend, you can release some of your tension.

If you don't have a specific, negative situation with which you're dealing, but your job is generally stressful spend time with other people outside of work. Instead of exercising by yourself or watching TV at home, set up a tennis or racquetball. Work out at a gym with a partner, hire a personal trainer for 30 minutes or drop in on an exercise class. Go out for dinner and drinks with a group of friends. Offer to babysit for friends. Pets can provide positive energy; consider pet sitting for a friend or walking an elderly neighbor's dog.

In some instances, you'll want to talk about work, such as with a partner, sibling or parent. In other situations, you'll want to simply spend time with others to take your mind off work.

# Alcohol, Tobacco and Drugs

Alcohol, tobacco and drugs aren't the main culprits in substance abuse. It's the reasons people use them that are the real problem.

You probably never hear people you know say, "My job is going great. I have plenty of money. My kids are wonderful. I have lots of friends. I need to get wasted!"

People lean on substances to help them deal with stress caused by work, relationships, money problems and other issues. If you have more than a social drink or two at a party, a glass of wine with dinner or are still smoking pot or using cocaine into adulthood, you may want to ask yourself why.

Even if you are not addicted to any substance, it might be a good idea to catalogue any you use and ponder scenarios in which you might turn to them for more than recreation. If your work scenario suddenly becomes desperate, or if your marriage goes south, do you know which substance you might most likely reach for to help relax you?

If so, it's a good idea to identify some red flags that will tell you that you may be headed toward substance abuse. If you begin drinking in the morning or alone. If you spend more money on drugs than normal. If you smoke only at work or home. These are signs you may be using substances to deal with stress, rather than trying to eliminate the stress.

People often drink, smoke or use other substances to deal with stress. Using substances to reduce stress doesn't eliminate or even reduce the stress-causing problem and can affect your body's ability to deal with stress later.

If you smoke or drink, note when you do it. Are you having a beer with friends at the game, a glass of wine with dinner or a cocktail at a social function, or are you pouring yourself a drink to deal with a stressful situation.

When are you more likely to light up a cigarette, when you're in a bar with acquaintances, while you're outside doing yard work, or when you're alone at home after a fight with someone, or at the office struggling with a work-related problem?

## To-Do Lists

Do you ever feel out of control at work? That no matter how much work you do, things still aren't getting done?

Lack of organization, planning and tracking deprives you of a clear picture of where you need to go and how you are doing.

To-do lists are an excellent way to give you a way to add control to your life. They tell you exactly what you need to get done and let you know how you are doing with a quick glance.

To-do lists give you a realistic assessment of the fact that you have accomplished some of your goals, and can alleviate stress by showing you that you are, in fact, getting things done.

To-do lists can also motivate you to stay on track by reminding you that you have unfinished work. This can help prevent you from starting new projects that can wait until later, fooling around on the computer or working too slowly.

To-do lists can add stress to your life if you create unrealistic lists or set unrealistic deadlines for completing them.

## Tips for Reducing Stress

•Get sufficient sleep and take naps
•Exercise three or more times per week
•Keep a daily journal
•Talk with people about everyday stresses
•Listen to relaxing music
•Avoid work and stressful TV shows at least one hour before bed
•Organize your day and week with a to-do list
•Reduce your intake of coffee, cigarettes, tea, soda, beer, wine and soda.

# Stress Questions

The more of these questions you answer, "Yes," the more likely you are creating stress in your life.

•Do you feel you are always late or behind schedule?

•Do you feel disorganized?

•Are you still angry about things that have happened in the past?

•Are you upset with friends, family members or business associates who do not know you are upset with them?

•Do you feel you have unhealthy eating habits?

•Do you dislike delegating, preferring to handle tasks yourself?

•Do you get irritated or angry easily or frequently?

•Do you share your feelings with someone, or keep to yourself?

•Do you exercise regularly?

•Do you regularly get enough sleep?

•Are you impatient with vendors, clients, customers or co-workers?

•Do you wait until deadline to finish projects?

•Do you feel your job is in jeopardy or your company is struggling?

•Do you have financial problems?

•Do you have relationship problems?

•Do you use alcohol or cigarettes to relieve stress?

# Chapter Summary

•Your thoughts stimulate the production of various chemicals that affect your body.

•Write a list of situations you know cause you stress.

•Identify signs that tell you a stressful situation is coming.

•Prepare responses to stressful situations.

•Rehearse your reaction to stressful situations.

•Use sports to expose yourself to control stressed and to practice stress-reducing techniques.

•Take a deep breath, hold it, and let it go slowly. Take a deep breath through your nose.

•Exercise at the end of a stressful day.

•Learn to mentally deal with traffic.

•Use family, friends and pets as stress-release valves.

•Analyze your use of alcohol, tobacco and drugs to determine when and why you use them.

•Use To-do lists to organize your day.

# Chapter 5:
# Managing the Flu
## (You're Going to Get it)

If you work in an office or fly commercially, you have a good chance of getting the flu each year.

After seniors and children, office workers may be the next most likely group to catch the flu annually, which not only whacks millions of people each year with considerable pain and illness, but kills thousands, as well. As much as 20 percent of the U.S. population gets the flu annually, with an estimated 200,000 Americans requiring hospitalization and thousands dying.

And we're not talking about the type of flu we got as kids that let us stagger into class or the office while fighting off our 24-hour bug. Today's flu strains are much more serious and are likely to badly slam you for a minimum of three days or last as long as a week. And there is more than one strain floating around each year.

You also may not be able to work from home as you suffer from headaches, high fever, sore throat, vomiting, diarrhea, deep coughing, chills and sore joints. If you're an attorney who bills $200 an hour, 10 hours a day, a three-day bout with the flu can cost your firm $6,000. If you make a $100,000 annual salary, you could lose more than $1,400 in paid time off if you're sick three days.

A $20 flu shot is conceivably the biggest no-brainer health investment a working professional can make. Additionally, it's a good idea to spend some money on flu meds and foods before you get sick — once you're very ill, you may not be able to get out of bed and go to the store for what you need, dragging your flu out longer than necessary and being sicker than you need to be.

# The Basics

What can you do once you get the flu? First, it's important to differentiate between <u>treating</u> the actual flu and <u>reducing</u> its symptoms.

According to expert sources like the Mayo Clinic and Centers for Disease Control and Prevention, the best way to <u>treat</u> he flu is simply to get plenty of rest and drink lots of fluids. This doesn't mean you can't do a variety of things to help alleviate symptoms and reduce your pain and suffering while you have the flu.

Some natural treatments make common sense, but may backfire, so it's best you consult a physician before trying any that go beyond rest, hydration and over-the-counter meds.

For example, mothers are told not to try and break a child's fever when he as the measles or chicken pox, because a fever is your body's way of trying to naturally kill germs by "burning" or "baking" them. Taking this logic, you might want to raise your thermostat, put on sweats, pile on the covers and try to raise your body temperature to kill your flu. However, this can lead to dehydration or a more severe fever, which can lead to brain damage.

Think of your brain like a raw egg. When you put it into a hot pan, the protein-rich yoke turns from bright yellow to a dull yellow as it heats up. When your protein-rich brain reaches a certain temperature, you can do permanent damage.

On the other hand, you can try to reduce your body temperature to feel better, lowering your home temperature, lying on top of your covers, drinking iced liquids, taking a tepid bath or using cold compresses on your forehead, ankles, knees, wrists and elbows. This may make you feel better, but fights your body's attempts to address your flu cause.

Before you attempt to regulate your body temperature, contact your personal physician, local doc-in-the-box or your pharmacy and ask for advice. Don't trust websites that seem to be authoritative unless they are connected with a hospital, university or government agency. Even then, you might misinterpret the data, so it's best to talk with a professional.

Some believe that light exercise can help you overcome the flu, raising your body temperature and releasing positive hormones. Depending on how severe your symptoms are, this could weaken you, and you might fall or otherwise injure yourself while exercising. While getting out of bed and walking around may help you clear your head and shake off some grogginess, you probably shouldn't get on an exercise machine without talking to a health professional first.

## What to Eat?

While you can choose foods that contain specific vitamins and minerals to try and target illnesses, once you have the flu, food and medicines, including much-touted vitamin C, won't cure you. Eating a balance of mild foods that won't upset your stomach and provide you with a good mix of complex carbohydrates, lean protein, vitamins and minerals is a sensible approach to eating when you have the flu, since it will help boost your immune system.

Fruits and fruit juices are a good source of healthy vitamins and minerals and contain significant amounts of water, helping you stay hydrated. They should not be your sole source of nutrition while you're sick, since you'll need your carbs and protein. Avoid fruit juices that are mostly water, sweeteners, additives and preservatives. Fresh or canned fruit are better choices than most commercial fruit juices. Bananas and kiwis are good sources of potassium, an important electrolyte you lose through sweating, vomiting and diarrhea.

Hot soups are another good choice when you have the flu, since they are also water-based and can provide you with carbs, proteins, vitamins and minerals. Soups can help clear congestion because of the steam rising off the dish. Researchers aren't exactly sure why, but chicken soup seems to have an additional benefit beyond other hot liquids in helping reduce mucus production and inflammation, so consider regular doses of this "Jewish penicillin."

If you are having a serious problem with congestion, avoid dairy products, which can increase mucus production.

Good carb choices include rice, dry toast, soda crackers, tortillas, mashed potatoes and oatmeal.

If you have vomiting or diarrhea, avoid heavy, spicy foods. Stick with soda crackers, ginger ale, consommé or broth, mashed potatoes and gelatin. Doctors often recommend the BRAT diet when you have the flu – bananas, rice, applesauce and toast. These foods are easily digestible if you're having stomach problems. Fruit and fruit juice may seem mild, but can have citric acid, which can cause stomach problems.

## Sports Drinks

When you have the flu, you lose not only water, but also electrolytes, such as salt, potassium and magnesium. Have you ever had very thin saliva with a tinny taste? If so, you're probably lacking in electrolytes. Sports drinks like Gatorade are specifically designed not only to hydrate you, but also to reduce the electrolytes you lose through sweat. When you're sick, you lose more electrolytes through vomiting and diarrhea. Consider drinking a sports drink that provides you with carbohydrates and electrolytes.

Stay away from coffee, tea and caffeinated drinks that can act as diuretics and further dehydrate you.

# Other Tips

**Medicate**
Don't take aspirin. Instead, relieve aches and pain with over-the-counter products that contain ibuprofen and acetaminophen, found in medications like Tylenol, Advil, and Motrin. Try lozenges to help your sore throat and syrups and drinks made to help reduce congestion.

**Gargle**
Gargle with warm salt water. You can immediately reduce the pain of a sore throat with a salt gargle.

**Sit Up**
Prop yourself up if you have a headache or congestion. This will help your sinuses drain better than if you lie flat.

**Shower**
A warm shower will relax your muscles and the steam will help decongest you. Turn your bathroom into a sauna by running the shower with the door closed. If you have a severe fever, be careful of raising your body temperature even further with a hot shower or bath.

**Spit**
When you cough up liquid, don't swallow it again. Your body is trying to get rid of it. Keep a container near your bed so you can discharge any phlegm or mucus that comes up. Don't keep this near you for days on end — rinse the container out each time you get up.

**Blow**
Blow your nose gently by doing so slowly, one nostril at a time, rather than by pressing against both nostrils and trying to use lots of pressure.

## Plug

Use nose plugs. Constantly sniffling mucus that is running from your nose back into your sinuses can increase the pressure in you head. Take a toilet paper square and rip it in half. Rip the remaining piece in half and roll the two pieces into small balls. Place them in your nose and let them catch any running mucus. These can last for hours or may need to be replaced frequently, depending on how fast your nose is running. If you put these in when you sleep, they can help you sleep peacefully for many hours; however, you'll be breathing through your mouth the entire time and may experience a sore throat when you awake. A quick salt-water garlic will help alleviate this soreness.

# Chapter Summary

•Businesspeople are a high-risk group for the flu. Millions of Americans get the flu each year, with more than 200,000 hospitalized and thousands of death.

•You cannot cure the flu, only treat it and reduce some symptoms.

•Rest and fluids are the best two ways to treat the flu.

•You can reduce many symptoms with nutrition, over-the-counter meds and a few other tips for making yourself more comfortable.

•Have flu meds available in your home before you get sick; once you're very sick, you aren't likely to get out of bed and go to the store.

•Eat mild foods that give you a good mix of complex carbs, lean protein and vitamins and minerals.

•Some sports drinks replace electrolytes you lose sweating, vomiting and going to the bathroom.

•Don't try to raise or lower your body temperature without talking to a doctor first.

•Gargle with warm salt water to relieve a sore throat.

•Don't fly or go into work for at least two days after your fever breaks.